To Mend: Seeds Are Sewn

vol. 1

hem

Made with ❤ on the BookLeaf Publishing Platform
www.bookleafpub.in
www.bookleafpub.com

Dedication

dedicated to loose ends, worn and tired, gardens along cuticles and nail beds, watering can clouds above heads, mud betwixt toes, frayed edges folks. let worries become seeds and plant them elsewhere. roots meant for you will grow to hold you together.

Preface

before seeds, before trees, before earth, before water, before the sun - all was darkness whispering. listen, then open your eyes, deep breath and stretch. feed and water self and garden. move and be still with equal purpose. keep tidy body and mind. explore creation and creating. seek balance, know calm. be kind, accept love. stay true, curious and learning. observe discontent. meditate and heal every time. run toward fear. become new. love, love, and love.

Acknowledgements

to all who teach, to all who choose to learn, to those who have taught me with such immeasurable grace, seemingly outweighing my potential, thank you for upholding me as a possibility. to anyone i have ever had the privilege of expressing my love to, your lessons in my life are inseparable from me now. choosing honor as the thread to mend through love is to be endlessly blessed. and to those we all have not yet loved, you're part of the mending too.

one. [1]

do remember
to stitch love
into the hymn
of yourself
every
day.

two. [2]

seeds are sewn
with room to grow
with these words
i'm building a home.
a steady foundation,
a steady hand,
a steadfast heart.
i cannot fail you.
roots are threads
between stars
and rivers,
caverns
and chambers,
my heart
and yours.

three. [3]

trauma-informed patience,
i will wait, you are worth the waiting,
i thought.
it wasn't meant to be seen,
the fall.
then sinking
further into the floor,
further into my own hands again,
where i used to write 'remember'
along my forearms, teenage tattoos.
to be good and marked as such.
as a kid with a memory that burned me to form,
there is no forgetting some things.
so, please, please remember,
i am made of light,
i'll surface soon, where light is,
where pain is not,
i'm certain.

trauma-informed patience,
i am worth the healing, i thought.

four. [4]

have you ever seen the world?
on the other side of hell
is heaven.
on the other side
of any thing
is that which it is not.
all the while,
if it could have been,
it can be still.
so should your hell precede your heaven,
the rest awaits your seeing.

five. [5]

you can say to me
all the things
you need to see
on someone else
instead of yourself.

i can understand
how you can't stand
the things that
you don't know
about you,
but i don't doubt
you can learn
to love.

you can't convince a person to follow you into
themselves.

six. [6]

yes, it must take
exactly
this
much
pressure
for a person to realize their beauty.

with no difference
of seed and soil
below a surface,
break ground.

seven. [7]

don't you know it's good to cry?
it only shows
you've got electricity
on the inside.

the seeds of our intention
bear fruit
only their gardeners are capable of harvesting.

eight. [8]

yves and atoms,
and letting go of sadness,
take my heart,
a gift to have,
a gift to give,
a gift to grow again.

nine. [9]

it's no mystery
plants with the worst taste
the most thorns
vast roots
and those that imitate
enjoy the quickest survival

ten. [10]

cultivate
love in place of work
nurture
patterns from once problems
transmute
truce for truth instead

give water for the flowers in your head.

eleven. [11]

for the tendency
of feeling like home
for every soul
but your own
proves
your garden grows
proves
you aren't alone
proves
your seeds, their seeds
sown.

twelve. [12]

to feel life
like a sunrise
to feel love
like creation
changes through seasons

love notes light the sky
the glow between
being endless pages
every secret and shame
of past love and tragedy
has a safe place

the weight
of your warmth
on my chest
holds me here
only ever loving you

thirteen. [13]

rose-colored glasses
perhaps you see
everything is flowering
and what could be
so wrong about that?

fourteen. [14]

i forgive myself
for all the hearts
i painted blue
like my own
if i hadn't been
keeping my chin up
for so long,
i might know another color,
but the sky,
it keeps me company.

fifteen. [15]

once,
all i wanted to be
was the space between
the hurt and the heavens.
in the mirror
my blues fill up
with liquid glass
but you can't crash through water,
we only enter.

sixteen. [16]

perhaps the fruit
is not only for us.
even in tending,
in pruning, and watering,
feeding with our hunger in mind,
how much of the harvest
is solely yours?

seventeen. [17]

and after every rain
i'm reminded
of how the flowers grow
where their roots'
intentions go
the further the reach,
the more actual
is the potential.

eighteen. [18]

may you see
the love you have grown
surround you.
to feel myself
wrapping
around your finger,
the privilege
of holding
such sacred space
on mine.

nineteen. [19]

meet me
in the daylight
when the sun is so high,
it is unbelievable
that it's the nearest star.
you are
the nearest heaven.

twenty. [20]

i am a well.
should you fall in,
i will lift you up,
with the weight
of all that fills me,
to ensure you
of your freedom.

twenty one. [21]

i am hem,
i was born this way,
sewn carefully into the split vale,
likeness of handmade sundress,
of pillowcase,
lightness of fruit trees,
hugging my own knees,
bathed in mother's milk,
until breaching, like prayer.

southern women know patience,
in passing wisdom,
the power in,
simple syllables, timing,
the weight of shamed crimson thread.
all this while, have bled and bled,
and cried and shed, and here
is where the walking led -
lead heaviness of truth let us uplift,
lest we forget
our origins.

thank you momma,
for the eyes in the back of my head,

for the sight you dream for me still,
for bringing me into the world,
and lovingly threatening to take me back out.
thank you daddy,
for loving her from here to the heavens and back.

let me grow love like yours in southern soil.